Sex...
According to
God

STUDY GUIDE

KAY ARTHUR

with David & BJ Lawson

WATERBROOK
PRESS

SEX...ACCORDING TO GOD STUDY GUIDE
PUBLISHED BY WATERBROOK PRESS
2375 Telstar Drive, Suite 160
Colorado Springs, Colorado 80920
A division of Random House, Inc.

Quotations from *Sex...According to God* © 2002 by Kay Arthur

All Scripture quotations, unless otherwise indicated, are taken from the *New American Standard Bible®*. © Copyright The Lockman Foundation 1960, 1962, 1963, 1968, 1971, 1972, 1973, 1975, 1977, 1995. Used by permission. (www.Lockman.org)

ISBN 1-57856-640-1

Printed in the United States of America
2002—First Edition

10 9 8 7 6 5 4 3 2 1

Contents

Introduction

I'm so glad you've picked up this study guide, beloved. It's my heart's desire to see a new sexual revolution sweep our nation, but that won't happen until God's people open their eyes to the truths of His Word regarding sex—what's acceptable and what's not, the consequences of ignoring God's plan and the blessings of following His instructions.

The topic of the Creator's plan for sex is thoroughly covered in my book *Sex...According to God.* My hope, my desire is that you will find God's truth about sex so compelling that you will use *Sex...According to God* as a curriculum for a small group study. This companion study guide is designed to help your study group (teens or adults, single, married, divorced, or those living with a significant other) discuss the points raised in the book and apply what you've learned.

Designed with the teacher or facilitator in mind, this study guide follows the outline of each chapter in the primary book and covers the major scripture passages used, as well as occasionally referring to additional Bible passages. To provide context, I've included excerpts from *Sex...According to God* throughout this study guide, each of which is introduced with this symbol: 📖

The questions within each chapter are intended to stimulate discussion and provoke some soul searching among members of your group. Each lesson concludes with application questions that bring the ancient but unchanging truths of Scripture into our modern context.

You will recognize that some of the questions in this study guide are personal and challenging. These questions, geared to the individual reader, will not stimulate discussion, nor are they designed to. They are included to help the group leader challenge participants with the truths they are learning. As a leader, you, of course, have the freedom to use whatever questions you feel are appropriate for your group. This guide is a tool, not a teacher. Under the leadership of the Holy Spirit, you'll want to use the questions as needed to help lead the group into a relevant discussion of the often misunderstood subject of sex.

I pray you will find this tool helpful as you seek to understand God's will in this area and as you pass on to others the life-changing truths you discover as you learn about *Sex...According to God.*

Together, let's start a new sexual revolution!

~⌒

Sex Is Like a Can of Drano

A companion Bible study to the introduction
and chapter 1 in *Sex...According to God*

📖 I was still amazed at what an incredibly quick job Drano did on my sink. *What a great product!* I thought. *Read the directions, do what it tells you, and it works! And nothing dire happened because I followed the directions.* Then it hit me: *Lord, sex is like a can of Drano! It's a wonderful "product," does a great job, but you have to use it according to the Manufacturer's directions.*

THE MANUFACTURER

Who is the "Manufacturer" of sex? And how do we know this?

1. Read Genesis 1:25-28 (found on pages 10-11 in *Sex...According to God*), then discuss the following questions.

What do you learn about mankind from this passage?

Who is our "Manufacturer"?

In your experience, who defines what something is designed for? Who decides its specifications and limits?

From what you read in this passage, what is one of the reasons God created sex?

2. Read Genesis 2:7-8,15-25 (found on pages 12-13 in *Sex...According to God*), then discuss the following questions.

What do you learn about the creation of man and woman in this passage?

According to what you read in Genesis 1 and 2, are we created asexual or sexual?

What was God's purpose for creating woman?

Genesis 2:24 says the two shall become "one flesh." What does this mean?

Who is involved in becoming "one flesh"?

3. Read 1 Corinthians 6:15-18 (found on pages 15-16 in *Sex... According to God*).

From this passage, what additional insight(s) do you gain concerning "one flesh"?

⚲ If you want truth without distortion, you'll find it in the Bible. God's Book tells us we were created distinctively male and female. Eve was designed to be a suitable helper, a companion for Adam. Both were also designed for the purpose of procreation. Two men, no matter how they were raised, cannot have sex and produce a child. Neither can two women. It takes a sperm and an egg to make a child—and for those elements you need a man and woman.

Sex really is like a can of Drano. So let's take a little more time to look at the "Manufacturer's directions."

"READ BACK LABEL CAREFULLY"

Where would we go to learn about the Manufacturer's directions and warnings? In other words, if we're supposed to "read the label" to find out the proper use of sex, where will we find it?

4. Read the following four passages. For each one, ask as many of the "5 W's and an H" questions—Who, What, When, Where, Why, and How—as you possibly can. Discuss what you learn from each passage about truth and the Word?

So Jesus was saying to those Jews who had believed Him, "If you continue in My word, then you are truly disciples of Mine; and you will know the truth, and the truth will make you free." (John 8:31-32)

The works of His hands are truth and justice; all His precepts are sure. They are upheld forever and ever; they are performed in truth and uprightness. He has sent redemption to His people; He has ordained His covenant forever; holy and awesome is His name. The fear of the LORD is the beginning of wisdom; a good understanding have all those who do His commandments; His praise endures forever. (Psalm 111:7-10)

You are near, O LORD, and all Your commandments are truth. (Psalm 119:151)

Sanctify them in the truth; Your word is truth. (John 17:17)

"POISON: MAY CAUSE BLINDNESS"

When it comes to sex, could violating the Manufacturer's directions really cause blindness?

5. Read the following passages. What do you learn from each one about a spiritual state of blindness—specifically its cause and/or its cure?

> I will bring distress on men so that they will walk like the
> blind, because they have sinned against the LORD; and
> their blood will be poured out like dust. (Zephaniah 1:17)

The Spirit of the LORD is upon Me, because He anointed
Me to preach the gospel to the poor. He has sent Me to
proclaim release to the captives, and recovery of sight to the
blind, to set free those who are oppressed, to proclaim the
favorable year of the LORD. (Luke 4:18-19)

"GIVE FIRST AID"

6. What do you learn from each of the following passages about the
   damaging effects of sin—its cause and/or its cure?

   For the brokenness of the daughter of my people I am
   broken; I mourn, dismay has taken hold of me. Is there no
   balm in Gilead? Is there no physician there? Why then has
   not the health of the daughter of my people been restored?
   (Jeremiah 8:21-22)

(In the previous passage from Jeremiah 8, we read that the people had not been healed because they had not applied the "balm of Gilead" and had not cried to the Great Physician. We know God is the Great Physician, but what is the balm of Gilead? Gilead was an area known for an ointment, which, when applied to the skin, had healing properties.)

If we confess our sins, He is faithful and righteous to forgive us our sins and to cleanse us from all unrighteousness. (1 John 1:9)

Fools, because of their rebellious way, and because of their iniquities, were afflicted. Their soul abhorred all kinds of food, and they drew near to the gates of death. Then they cried out to the LORD in their trouble; He saved them out of their distresses. He sent His word and healed them, and delivered them from their destructions. (Psalm 107:17-20)

According to the verses from Psalm 107, what was the cause of the people's affliction?

What did God send to cure them?

What was their responsibility in the healing process?

What is our responsibility today in the healing process?

Is "first aid" of this kind available today? Where can we find it?

HOW DOES THIS APPLY TODAY?

7. What are some of the pressures your peers face today with respect to their sexuality?

8. How aware do you think people are of what God's Book, the Bible, has to say about our sexuality? Why do you suppose this is?

9. According to what you learned this week, what would you tell a person to do if he or she had broken God's commandments regarding sex, and he or she wanted to be forgiven—to change?

Portrait of a Virgin

A companion Bible study to chapter 2

in *Sex...According to God*

📖 If marriage is a metaphor of God's union with Israel, and
He calls Israel a harlot because of her unfaithfulness...and if it's
a metaphor of the church as Christ's bride, and God calls her
an adulteress because of her friendship with the world...then
what value does God place on our virginity as women or men?

THE GIFT OF A LIFETIME

What value does God place on our virginity?

1. Read Deuteronomy 22:13-21 (found on pages 23-24 in
   Sex...According to God), then discuss the following questions.

What do you learn about the word *virgin* from this passage?

What was the consequence for publicly defaming a virgin of Israel?

If the charge was true and the girl was found not to be a virgin, what was the consequence? Why was this to be done?

What does this indicate about how seriously God takes virginity?

A FRAGILE BEAUTY

    📖 We see on television and in other forms of "entertainment" the excitement, the desire, the passion, the pleasure of sex, but we rarely see it in the context where it belongs, within the confines of marriage....

    What does God intend?... "For whom is sex intended?"

    This question needs to be answered with every generation. Although God's "moral production code" never changes, our culture does.... So each generation needs to hear what God says.

2. Read Genesis 2:22-25 (found on page 29 in *Sex...According to God*), then discuss the following questions.

Who made woman? How was she made?

What was man's response to God's creation?

At what point did the commitment come—before or after the sex?

According to this passage, for whom does sex seem to be intended?

3. What do you learn about marriage from the following New Testament passage?

> Marriage is to be held in honor among all, and the marriage bed is to be undefiled; for fornicators and adulterers God will judge. (Hebrews 13:4)

THE WAYS OF A MAN

📕 People have thought for generations that the woman is to remain a virgin until marriage, but not the man. Is that true? *After all,* you may be thinking, *he's a man! And men—well, because they're men, they have to have sex!...* But what does God say?

4. Read Proverbs 5:15-23 (found on page 32 in *Sex...According to God*).

In light of the context of this passage, what is the father warning the son against?

What is the implication for us today?

5. Read 1 Corinthians 7:1-2,8-9 (found on page 34 in *Sex...According to God*), then discuss the following questions.

Where are our sexual desires to be met? Why?

What is the message to those who are single or widowed?

If a man is burning with sexual desire, what is the solution? Why? What would this tell you about God's view of virginity with respect to men?

HOW DOES THIS APPLY TODAY?

6. What would your peers say about the scriptures on virginity?

What would keep them from listening to or respecting God's Word on this subject? How would you answer them at this point?

7. What are some questions—or feelings—people will have to deal with if they don't save themselves sexually for their spouse?

The following question is one to answer only in your mind—unless you're in a group of the same sex and you feel you can trust and help one another. If you do decide to share, then pray for one another and hold one another accountable before God. Remember Galatians 6:1-2:

> Brethren, even if anyone is caught in any trespass, you who
> are spiritual, restore such a one in a spirit of gentleness; each
> one looking to yourself so that you too will not be tempted.
> Bear one another's burdens, and thereby fulfill the law of
> Christ.

8. Have you touched another person in such a way as to arouse him or her sexually? In your lust, have you defrauded another, have you violated their virginity simply to satisfy your desires? If so, what does God say about it?

Caution: Sex Can Be Dangerous

A companion Bible study to chapter 3

in *Sex...According to God*

📖 God says more about the negative side of sex than about the positive side. Why? Simply because He's a gracious and loving God, and He doesn't want you to be burned, bruised, broken, disillusioned, and scarred for life because you listened to the philosophy of men. Our loving Father is brokenhearted that so many have dived headfirst into the shimmering sea of sex, become caught in the undercurrent of the culture, and now find themselves gasping for air as they go down for the second time. He offers in His Word the lifeline, the rescue from certain death.

THE CONSEQUENCES OF SEX OUTSIDE OF MARRIAGE

1. Read Deuteronomy 22:22-29 (found on pages 40-41 in *Sex...According to God*), then discuss the following questions.

What does God have to say about sex outside of marriage?

What are the consequences of violating God's standard?

What is God's reason for putting these people to death?

According to God, what is the evil that is to be purged?

GOD'S RIGHTEOUS JUDGMENT FOR SEXUAL SIN

2. Reread Deuteronomy 22:22-29 (pages 40-41 in *Sex...According to God*). Discuss the first three scenarios described in this passage.

What is God's judgment in each scenario? Why?

How would the enforcement of God's punishment today protect women from rape?

How is the fourth scenario different?

What does this indicate about how seriously God takes the marriage covenant?

Why do you think we don't we take it as seriously?

3. Look again at the following passage from Hebrews, and see how the message compares to what we have seen so far.

> Marriage is to be held in honor among all, and the marriage
> bed is to be undefiled; for fornicators and adulterers God
> will judge. (Hebrews 13:4)

What does God say in this verse about sex outside of marriage? What right does He have to say something like this?

Has God's position changed from the Old Testament to the New Testament concerning sex outside of marriage? Is His position different today?

What difference should knowing this make in our lives?

4. Read Exodus 22:16-17 (found on page 45 in *Sex...According to God*).

In God's Law, is a virgin always required to marry the man who took her virginity?

According to these verses, what is the alternative to marriage?

What would be the attitude of your peers about this today?

THE QUESTION OF SAFE SEX

📖 According to God, is there any such thing as safe sex if you're not married? It's a valid question in light of a culture that really doesn't know what God says on the subject, isn't it?

5. In this portion of chapter 3 in *Sex...According to God,* you read background information about the Greco-Roman world. How is our society similar?

In what ways are we different?

What danger(s) does this pose for us as a society today?

6. Read 1 Thessalonians 4:1-8 (found on pages 49-50 in *Sex... According to God*). Let's interrogate the text by asking the following questions and see what we learn.

What did the Thessalonians receive from Paul, and why?

What is the will of God for the Thessalonians?

What is God's will for you today?

What do you learn about sanctification in these verses?

What does this passage teach us about sex?

What does this passage teach about defrauding others?

How will knowing this affect your behavior in the future?

HOW DOES THIS APPLY TODAY?

7. Consider recent news events focusing on individuals whose lives reflect disregard for God's plan for sex. What consequences, if any, have they experienced for violating God's Law?

Are there people you know personally who have had problems because they violated God's Law? What consequences, if any, did they experience?

Based upon what you have learned so far, how do you feel about safe sex?

8. Do you really believe that God will judge every person if they violate His standards regarding sex? Give the reason for your answer.

What do you think is our responsibility to others when we know they are breaking God's Law with respect to sex?

What have you learned about God that would help anyone who has gone against His commandments?

📖 Paul is giving the Thessalonians—and you and me—fair warning.... He's letting us know that we can't go against God's Word in the sphere of sex and get away with it.

LESSON 4

Beware of Taking
Forbidden Fruit

A companion Bible study to chapter 4

in *Sex...According to God*

  The Law not only set boundaries to protect and restrain people, it also defined unacceptable behavior and set forth the consequences of choosing to transgress God's holy commandments.... As with any responsible manufacturer, God put warnings on the label and described what was to be done if they weren't heeded.

GOD'S PERSPECTIVE ON ADULTERY AND COVETOUSNESS

1. From Exodus 20:14,17 (found on page 57 in *Sex...According to God*), what do you learn about adultery?

According to God, what constitutes adultery?

What does it mean to "covet" your neighbor's wife or husband?

Take a moment to reflect honestly on your thought life and actions. Have you ever or are you now violating one of these commandments? (Once again, share this only in a group setting where you have trust and mutual accountability.)

2. Read the following passage from Proverbs, and note what happens when a man allows himself to be enticed by a woman.

> Do not desire her beauty in your heart, nor let her capture you with her eyelids. For on account of a harlot one is reduced to a loaf of bread, and an adulteress hunts for the precious life. Can a man take fire in his bosom and his clothes not be burned? Or can a man walk on hot coals and his feet not be scorched? So is the one who goes in to his neighbor's wife; whoever touches her will not go unpunished. (Proverbs 6:25-29)

According to verse 25, where does adultery start? Where does it lead?

What are the consequences, if any?

3. Read the following scripture.

You have heard that it was said, "You shall not commit adultery"; but I say to you that everyone who looks at a woman with lust for her has already committed adultery with her in his heart. (Matthew 5:27-28)

Is it okay for a man to look as long as he doesn't touch? Why?

4. In Exodus 20:18-20 (found on page 58 in *Sex...According to God*), you learned that the Commandments were a test.

What do you think that means?

How would they test you?

WHAT ELSE IS FORBIDDEN?

5. Read Leviticus 20:7-8 (found on page 60 in *Sex...According to God*).

   What are God's people told to do? Why?

6. According to Leviticus 20:10-22 (found on pages 60-63 in *Sex...
   According to God*), what is forbidden? What are the consequences
   for disobedience?

📖 So what is forbidden in these verses? Adultery. Incest.
Homosexuality. Bestiality. It's quite a lineup, isn't it? But are
they problems today? All of them? Yes, they're often friends,
calling each other to join their salacious party. Each is being
practiced today in ways and forms you and I probably could
never conceive of.

HOPE FOR THE CAPTIVE

7. In 1 Corinthians 6:9-11 (found on page 65 in *Sex...According to God*), what did you learn from marking *you* and *were*?

What is the message of hope in this passage?

What does the Lord Jesus do for *you* according to this passage?

8. In chapter 4 you're referred to another passage of hope and encouragement: Romans 5:6-11. Read this passage and discuss the questions that follow.

> For while we were still helpless, at the right time Christ died
> for the ungodly. For one will hardly die for a righteous man;
> though perhaps for the good man someone would dare even
> to die. But God demonstrates His own love toward us, in
> that while we were yet sinners, Christ died for us. Much
> more then, having now been justified by His blood, we shall
> be saved from the wrath of God through Him. For if while
> we were enemies we were reconciled to God through the
> death of His Son, much more, having been reconciled, we

shall be saved by His life. And not only this, but we also exult in God through our Lord Jesus Christ, through whom we have now received the reconciliation.

What did God do for us while we were sinners, when we were ungodly and helpless?

By doing this, what did God demonstrate?

How does this truth apply today?

COURTING GOD'S JUDGMENT

9. Read Leviticus 18:22-30 (found on pages 67-68 in *Sex...According to God*).

What sins does God characterize with the terms *abomination* and *perversion*?

Look at every place in this passage where you marked the words *defile* or *defiled*. What did you learn?

According to verses 24 and 28, does God deal only with His chosen people with respect to their sins, or does He expect obedience from everyone?

What were the children of Israel to do according to verse 26?

What would be the result of their obedience? of their disobedience?

According to this passage, what does God desire for us?

DESTROYED BY A LIE

📖 Can you see how essential it is that we understand exactly what God says about sex? If we don't understand it, we'll be deceived and destroyed by a lie. Beloved, sex outside God's parameters is a forbidden fruit that will keep you out of His garden, the only place you will find the Tree of Life.

10. Read Psalm 32:3-10 (found on page 72 in *Sex...According to God*).

What happened when the psalmist kept silent about his sin?

When we experience similar conviction, how should we respond?

What do you learn about God in these verses?

What is being contrasted in the last two lines of this passage?

📖 Regardless of who you are, your sins will find you out.
God is a holy God; He must judge sin. Guilt, shame, and a
nagging conscience are precursors to impending judgment,
warning signs to stop and experience God's cleansing power
before it's too late.

HOW DOES THIS APPLY TODAY?

11. Why does sex so often bring shame and guilt?

12. What is God's perspective on adultery?

How is our society's perspective different? In what ways is this seen?

13. When it comes to sex, are there any parallels between covetousness
and adultery? Explain.

What are ways we could covet our neighbor's spouse without committing adultery?

14. Is God's perspective on sex the same today, or has He changed his mind?

15. What hope is there for someone caught in this web of sin? How would you counsel such a person?

The Snare of Seduction

A companion Bible study to chapter 5

in *Sex...According to God*

📖 Proverbs, written by King Solomon of Israel, is a textbook of wisdom and instruction that urged his son to flee from the evil woman, from the smooth tongue of the adulteress. As Circe warned Odysseus, so Solomon warned his son. But the wisdom offered by Solomon was God's wisdom—truth, not myth—counsel sent from the very throne of heaven.

WHAT'S THE BIG DEAL ABOUT SOWING A FEW WILD OATS?

1. Read Proverbs 6:20-29 (found on pages 74-75 and 77 in *Sex... According to God*).

What did you learn by marking each reference to *commandments*?

In this passage what is the son urged to do? How would it benefit him?

Just so you don't miss it, according to verses 23 and 24, what is the benefit of obedience?

What are the results of disobedience?

Have you followed your own desires rather than the teaching of the Word?

If you are a parent, what are you doing or what can you do to teach your children the commandments of the Lord in order to protect them from ignorance and possible ruin?

THE RISK AND REWARD OF OBEDIENCE

God didn't just record His commandments, He gave us a role model—
Joseph!

2. Discuss what you learned from Joseph's experience with Potiphar's
   wife described in Genesis 39:7-9 (found on page 78 in *Sex...
   According to God*).

   How did Joseph's relationship with the Lord affect his choices?

   What do you learn about Mrs. Potiphar in this passage? How did
   she deal with her desires?

   If someone pressures you to have sex outside of God's design, what
   should your answer be? Why? How do you think it would impact
   that person? How might he or she react? How would you explain
   your reason?

3. Read Genesis 39:19-20 (found on page 79 in *Sex...According to God*) to see the consequences of Joseph's choice.

What was Potiphar's response to his wife's accusations?

In what ways could you suffer for doing what is right?

Are you willing to suffer rejection, the ridicule of men, perhaps even loneliness for doing what is right? What does God promise in Matthew 5:10 and 1 Peter 3:12-14 to those who are willing to suffer?

THE WOUNDS OF SEXUAL SIN

4. According to Proverbs 6:30-35 (found on page 79 in *Sex...According to God*), what do you learn about someone who commits adultery?

What is the result of adultery?

5. In the following passage, what is God's instruction, and why is it given?

> Flee immorality. Every other sin that a man commits is out-
> side the body, but the immoral man sins against his own
> body. (1 Corinthians 6:18)

Remember the wounds you saw in the Proverbs 6 passage in the previous question? Think about it. Discuss what the connection might
be between those wounds and this passage from 1 Corinthians.

Did you learn anything new from this passage regarding sexually
transmitted diseases? How do you think this information might affect
people's thinking about the ramifications of sex outside of marriage?

6. Discuss the sexual activity described in this passage:

> For this reason God gave them over to degrading passions;
> for their women exchanged the natural function for that
> which is unnatural, and in the same way also the men aban-
> doned the natural function of the woman and burned in
> their desire toward one another, men with men committing
> indecent acts and receiving in their own persons the due
> penalty of their error. (Romans 1:26-27)

What connection is there between this passage from Romans and the passages from Proverbs and 1 Corinthians in the two previous questions?

7. According to Proverbs 3:13-18 (found on pages 81-82 in *Sex...According to God*), what do you learn about wisdom?

How does this apply to what we have seen so far?

AS AN OX TO SLAUGHTER

8. Read Proverbs 7:1-10 (found on pages 82-83 in *Sex...According to God*), and discuss what Solomon is exhorting his son to do.

What does Solomon want his son's relationship to wisdom and understanding to be? Why?

What do you learn about the young man whom Solomon was watching?

How about you? Have you ever tried to use darkness to cover your actions? If so, what were the results?

9. According to Proverbs 7:11-23 (found on pages 84-86 in *Sex... According to God*), how does Solomon describe the adulterous woman?

What does she say or do to entice a "dumb" man? What are her tactics? Do you see anything like this today? Explain.

What will his foolishness cost him? Would it cost the same today?

What similarities, if any, do you see between the adulterous woman
and those around you?

10. Read Proverbs 7:24-27 (found on page 88 in *Sex...According to
God*). What is the message of this passage for us today?

     📖 If you want out, if you want to change, God will change
you. He can take up residence within, bringing His Son and
His Spirit. All you have to do is ask God to move in, and He
will give you the wisdom and power to say "No!" to sin and
walk away from it in His strength.

STRANGE WOMEN AND DUMB MEN

11. What do you learn in Proverbs 6:20–7:27 (found on pages 85-86
and 88 in *Sex...According to God*) about the "dumb" man?

12. Read Proverbs 5:3-4 (found on page 90 in *Sex...According to God*).
What additional insight does this passage give you concerning the
adulteress?

13. According to the following proverb, what is the attitude of the adulterous woman?

> This is the way of an adulterous woman: She eats and wipes her mouth, and says, "I have done no wrong." (Proverbs 30:20)

📖 When we replaced the "outdated" Word of God with the "scientific" research of man, we were blindsided by the devil. We unwittingly bought the murderer's lie. We ate the forbidden fruit without realizing we were banishing ourselves from the garden. In our exile we are missing out on the joy and security not only of virtue but also of family and, consequently, a safe and healthy society where women and children are valued and protected, where they can walk and play in the streets without fear.

HOW DOES THIS APPLY TODAY?

So, what's the big deal about sowing a few wild oats?

14. What lessons do you learn from the life of Joseph that can be applied today?

15. What have you learned from chapter 5 in *Sex...According to God* about sexually transmitted diseases and how prevalent they are today?

What are the possible connections between sexually transmitted diseases, our society's attitude towards sex, and the passages you studied this week?

16. What are the characteristics of someone "void of sense"? How could you recognize someone like that today?

17. What can we do to train our children in the Word of God so that they can recognize "dumb men" and "strange women"?

What do you need to do as a parent to ensure that your children do not become "dumb men" or "strange women"?

18. What can you do to avoid "strange women" or keep from becoming a "dumb" man?

LESSON 6

Consider the Cost

A companion Bible study to chapter 6
in *Sex...According to God*

📖 Do you find yourself relating to David? Have you seen a
beautiful woman you can't get out of your mind? Or are you
attracted to a particular man? Do you find yourself tempted,
ready to toss caution aside for the sake of fulfilling your
desires? If so, I urge you to postpone your decision until you
finish this book. You need to understand the gravity of your
actions. You need to consider your future.

THE PATH TO SIN

What leads us into temptation, and from temptation into sin? If we knew
the cause of events, then we could "flee" rather than end up "messing up."

1. Read Genesis 3:1-8 (found on pages 98-99 in *Sex...According to
   God*), and discuss the progression of events that brought sin into
   the world.

According to what you read, do you believe Eve knew what she was doing was wrong? What leads you to this conclusion?

2. Examine the progression of sin as found in Joshua 6:17-18 and 7:20-21 (found on page 100 in *Sex...According to God*).

   How does the progression here compare with what you saw in Genesis 3?

   How do you know Achan was consciously violating the Lord's commands?

3. In 2 Samuel 11:1-5 (found on page 97 in *Sex...According to God*), what were the choices made by David, king of Israel?

4. What is the path of sin as seen in the three preceding passages of Scripture?

What are some ways we can avoid taking this path?

What safeguards could you build into your life based on this truth you have seen?

THE WEB OF DECEIT

5. Read 2 Samuel 11:6-22 (found on pages 101-104 in *Sex...According to God*).

What do you learn in this passage about Uriah?

What were the options available to David at this point?

What would a man or woman of integrity have done?

THE RIGHTEOUS JUDGE

📖 David's cover-up was complete. It wasn't exactly as he
planned, but he pulled it off. Now he could bring Bathsheba
to his house and sleep with her without fear of any reprisal....

    If only David had stopped to consider his future, if only
he had thought his actions through to their logical conclusion,
he would have realized that God would never let him get away
with sin.

6. Read the following passages, and discuss what you learn about God
from each one.

But if you will not do so, behold, you have sinned against
the LORD, and be sure your sin will find you out.
(Numbers 32:23)

For the ways of a man are before the eyes of the LORD, and
He watches all his paths. (Proverbs 5:21)

The eyes of the LORD are in every place, watching the evil
and the good. (Proverbs 15:3)

7. Read 2 Samuel 12:1-10 (found on pages 106-108 in *Sex...According
to God*).

What two things had David despised?

Take a moment to examine your life. Have you despised the Lord
or His Word? If so, in what way(s)?

THE CONSEQUENCES OF ADULTERY

8. According to 2 Samuel 12:10-14, what are the consequences David
would suffer from his sin?

What do you think about these consequences? Are they appropriate? Why or why not?

Which people were affected by the consequences of David's sin?

In what ways are innocent people today affected by the consequences of the sins of others?

9. In Ezekiel 16 (found on pages 114-115 in *Sex...According to God*), you saw the pain Israel's adultery caused God. What were the consequences of Israel's adultery?

HOW DOES THIS APPLY TODAY?

10. What is the path to sin we've seen in these passages?

How is knowing about this significant for us today?

11. When you're discreet, who are you really hurting?

In what ways do we try to be discreet today?

12. What have you learned about God in this lesson?

How does what you learned apply to us today?

13. Chapter 6 of *Sex...According to God* lists seven consequences of adultery (found on pages 110-115). Think through and discuss each one.

Perhaps the Lord has shown you some sin that you thought was covered up but really isn't. Take a few moments in prayer to confess your sin and the cover-up to the Lord. Ask Him what you need to do to right the wrong.

📖 Do you realize that every time we sin—we who call ourselves Christians—it racks up another victory for the Enemy? Our sin leads the world to believe "there's nothing to this 'God stuff.'" And this is a world God longs to bring to Himself! I'm sure you've heard the comments: "Christians aren't any different than us; they just have a lot more rules! What good does it do to be a Christian?"

The Value of Righteous Indignation

A companion Bible study to chapter 7

in *Sex...According to God*

 Remember, I'm not judging you. It's God Word that judges us all. I simply want to help you discover what God says about such behaviors in the hope that you will embrace the truth. When you do, God says He will save you from your bondage to sin...according to His mercy, by the washing of regeneration and renewing by the Holy Spirit.

THE SIN OF SODOM AND GOMORRAH

1. Read Genesis 19:1-13 (found on pages 122-123 in *Sex...According to God*), and discuss the following questions.

How did the men of Sodom respond to Lot as he tried to reason with them?

When the men of Sodom were struck blind, how did they respond? In other words, did the men see the error of their ways?

This sounds repetitive, but it is so important that you see the truth for yourself. From simply reading the text, what do you think was the abomination being committed in Sodom?

2. According to Ezekiel 16:49-50 (found on page 122 in *Sex... According to God*), what are the sins of Sodom?

What is the progression you see in this passage?

Some people say that God destroyed the city *only* because its people didn't care for the poor and needy. Basing your answer on Scripture, can this be true? Explain.

3. Read Leviticus 18:22-30 (found on pages 124-125 in *Sex...According to God*), and discuss the specific sins the word *abomination* is used to describe.

How does the use of the word *abomination* in Leviticus help explain the sins described in Ezekiel 16?

How seriously does God view these sins?

4. Read Jude 6-7 (found on page 126 in *Sex...According to God*), and discuss the sin committed by Sodom and Gomorrah.

How does Jude describe the sins committed in Sodom?

How does this compare to the incident as recorded in Genesis 19 (found on pages 122-123 in *Sex...According to God*)?

5. According to 2 Peter 2:4-10 (found on pages 127-128 in *Sex... According to God*), what do you learn about Sodom and Gomorrah?

From all that you have read in these passages, exactly what are the sins of Sodom and Gomorrah?

The truth is not always easy, is it? But it is always necessary.

ETERNAL CONSEQUENCES OF AN
IMMORAL LIFESTYLE

   📖 Remember that if you're involved in any form of sexual immorality, there is hope. You *can* be forgiven. You *can* change. You can be made new. You can start again. You can experience healing if you'll come to Jehovah-rapha, the Lord God who heals.

6. Read 1 Corinthians 6:9-11 (found on page 129 in *Sex...According to God*). What truths do you learn about the people of the church in Corinth?

7. Read Ephesians 5:5-6 and Revelation 21:8; 22:14-15 (found on page 130 in *Sex...According to God*).

What do these passages teach you about immorality?

   📖 It's important to understand that these sins describe the *lifestyle* of these people—*not* their temptations, their battles, or their slip-ups, but a willful lifestyle. These are lifestyles of choice. These people are without excuse before God. They have chosen death over life, when a compassionate, merciful God would have saved them had they not hardened their hearts.

8. From Romans 1:18-32 (found on pages 131-132 in *Sex...According to God*), what do you learn about the ungodly or unrighteous?

What sexual behaviors are mentioned in this passage?

Are these men and women without excuse? If so, why?

Remember the illustration from the introduction of *Sex...According to God*—that sex is like a can of Drano? Sex is great when used according to God's directions, but when we deviate...the result is disastrous. You've seen this truth by studying the Scriptures for yourself. How will you respond?

A TIME FOR ANGER

📖 I wonder if we can begin to comprehend the pain that has come because everyone did what was right in their own eyes rather than in God's eyes. God was not their ruler; *they* were!

9. Read these verses from two places in the book of Judges.

> In those days there was no king in Israel; every man did
> what was right in his own eyes. (Judges 17:6)

> In those days there was no king in Israel; everyone did what
> was right in his own eyes. (Judges 21:25)

What is the key phrase that is repeated in these passages?

In what ways does that phrase describe our day?

10. Read Judges 19:22-30 (found on pages 137-138 in *Sex...According to God*). How could this happen in Israel?

11. From what you learned in chapters 20 and 21 of Judges, discuss the devastating consequences of sin.

How expensive is sin?

What attitude of the people allowed this kind of sin to occur?

You have seen the truth. It is not always easy to accept, but the alternative is to believe a lie, and the consequences of that are far worse.

HOW DOES THIS APPLY TODAY?

12. Who are we to judge what others do? On what basis do we judge the behavior of others?

13. What does the Bible say about homosexual behavior?

Does this apply to society today? What leads you to this conclusion?

14. What are the consequences of an immoral lifestyle?

How do we see these consequences manifested in our society today?

15. In Judges we saw that everyone did what was right in his own eyes. How does this attitude compare with our world today?

What should we do about it?

L E S S O N   8

Stitching Up the Wounds

A companion Bible study to chapter 8

in *Sex...According to God*

What do you do when your experience with sex has happened in a way that is not according to God's plan, either
because you've done something you shouldn't have or because
someone violated you sexually? Is it really possible to recover
and get on with life?

THE HEALING BALM OF GRACE

1. Read Psalm 51 (found on pages 145-147 in *Sex...According to God*),
and discuss what you learned about God from these verses.

In verse 1, who does David cry out to?

What is David seeking healing from?

2. What did you learn about God's compassion in chapter 8 of *Sex...According to God*?

A CLEANSING OF THE SOUL

3. Read Psalm 51:2-6 (found on pages 149-150 in *Sex...According to God*).

What do you learn about David in this passage?

How do you believe David feels about his sin?

According to verse 2, what specifically is David asking for?

Who does he see his sin is ultimately against, and what does he acknowledge?

What about you? Have you realized your sin is against God, the One you have willfully disobeyed?

What would a person do to show that he or she accepts full responsibility for his or her actions?

4. Read the following verses from 1 John.

If we say that we have no sin, we are deceiving ourselves and the truth is not in us…. If we say that we have not sinned, we make Him a liar and His word is not in us. (1 John 1:8,10)

What do we learn about ourselves from these verses?

5. Read Psalm 51:7-11 (found on pages 151-152 in *Sex...According to God*), and discuss what this passage teaches you about God.

Compare verses 2 and 7. What is the image of forgiveness the psalmist is painting for us?

What do forgiveness and cleansing bring?

THE RETURN OF JOY

6. Read Psalm 51:12 (found on page 152 in *Sex...According to God*).

What is David's request in this verse?

How is it even possible for us to know the joy of the Lord?

How is it possible for our churches to know the joy of the Lord?

7. Read Psalm 51:13-17 (found on pages 152-153 in *Sex...According to God*).

What will be the result of David's restoration?

In what ways can our failures and restoration be a platform for ministry?

Are healing and cleansing available? How can you partake in this?

How can your life be an example of God's restorative and renewing power?

THOSE AFFECTED BY YOUR SIN

8. Read Proverbs 6:32-35 (found on page 155 in *Sex...According to God*).

What are the results of adultery according to this passage?

What are some of the ways others are affected by our sin?

WHEN YOU ARE THE VICTIM

📖 Perhaps you've been misused sexually—abused, raped, betrayed.... What do you do when the sexual transgression has been against you? Beloved, you have a choice to make. You can be bitter, you can be angry, you can rage, you can hate, you can seek revenge—yet none of these will ever take care of the person's sin against you. Instead of punishing the perpetrator, you will punish only yourself—and once again become that person's victim. If you choose to handle it God's way, you'll know a healing and freedom you may never have thought you would experience again.

9. Look at the following verses from Psalms and Jeremiah:

> He sent His word and healed them, and delivered them
> from their destructions. (Psalm 107:20)

> Heal me, O LORD, and I will be healed; save me and I will
> be saved, for You are my praise. (Jeremiah 17:14)

According to these verses, where is healing found?

How would these verses help someone who was hurting because of sin—their own sin or someone else's?

10. Read 1 John 1:4-10 (found on pages 160-161 in *Sex…According to God*). What does this passage teach you…

about God?

about ourselves?

HOW DOES THIS APPLY TODAY?

11. From your studies this week, discuss how someone can be forgiven for their sins.

12. Receiving forgiveness and cleansing from God does not mean that there are no consequences for our actions.

    What are some of the consequences of sin we might have to deal with individually, even if we are forgiven?

    What are some of the consequences of sin we deal with as a society?

13. Is healing even possible today? What options for healing does the world offer?

What does God say? What manner of healing does He offer?

14. How would you share the healing grace of God with someone?

15. How does the Word of God cleanse?

Does the world offer cleansing? forgiveness? Or does it pass the blame, offer excuses or cover-ups?

📖 Can you see how important, how imperative it is that sin be recognized and confessed as sin? God says that those who cover their sins will never prosper. Without confession, there can be no healing. Therefore it's crucial that sin be exposed. It needs to be brought out in the open and dealt with accordingly.

In the Heat of the Moment

A companion Bible study to chapter 9

in *Sex...According to God*

What do we do with the temptation? How do we handle the passion that taunts our minds and burns in our bodies? What about the conversation in our mind, the inner voice that insists we're incapable of resisting the desires of our flesh? Is it really possible to resist, to win the battle against such inherent desires, to not yield to this natural longing for touch, for expression, for satisfaction?

TURNED ON

What do we do? What does God expect? How do we handle our desires, our sexual appetites?

1. As you studied the story of Amnon and Tamar in 2 Samuel 13 (found on pages 164-175 in *Sex...According to God*), what did you learn about the progression of sin?

Most of us can identify with Amnon. Is there someone you can't get out of your mind? Left unchecked, where will this thought pattern lead?

2. What life principles can you take away from the story of Amnon and Tamar concerning...

corrupt companions (Jonadab)?

receiving and acting on advice (Amnon)?

parenting sons?

parenting daughters?

SIN NEVER SATISFIES

3. From what you have studied so far, what does God say about what Amnon was proposing?

What tells you that Amnon knew what he was proposing was wrong?

Tamar wanted Amnon to wait. What might have been the outcome if Amnon had waited?

In what ways do we face the demand for instant gratification in our society?

How can a person resist these demands?

After Amnon raped Tamar, how did he respond to her?

What is the life principle we can take away from this story?

4. From James 1:13-17 (found on page 175 in *Sex...According to God*), what do you learn about being tempted or enticed?

According to this passage, how does sin progress?

In what ways did you see this progression in the story of Amnon and Tamar?

THE DEVIL'S DESIGN—AND OUR WAY OUT

5. Read Ephesians 2:1-6 (found on page 181 in *Sex...According to God*).

What were these people formerly, before God in His love saved them?

Personalize it. What were you before God saved you?

Verse 4 starts with a contrast. What is being contrasted?

What are we now as a result of God's great love?

6. Read Ephesians 5:3-12 (found on pages 182-183 in *Sex...According to God*).

What did you learn as you charted the difference between the children of Light and the sons of disobedience?

If you are a child of Light, do you have the ability to control your urges? Explain your answer from Scripture.

📖 Did you read those verses carefully? They're full of instruction aren't they? Why? Because these words are written to those who, according to Ephesians 2:1-6, are no longer children of wrath, walking according to...Satan, the prince of the power of the air. Those who receive these words are no longer bound to the standards or dictates of the world that lies under Satan's power.

AN ACTION PLAN

    📖 If your attraction to a particular person is drawing you toward sin, avoid going where you know he or she will be. If you have to pass by that person's home or office, don't look. Don't cruise the neighborhood. Change dentists, doctors, lawyers, pastors, secretaries, accountants—whatever it takes to avoid whoever is attracting you.

7. Read 1 Corinthians 6:13-20 (found on pages 185-186 in *Sex…According to God*).

From this passage, what did you learn about the body?

If your body is the temple of the Holy Spirit, what are the ramifications of this?

According to verse 18, who does the immoral man sin against? In what ways?

Now that we have studied this passage, how far can you go with someone to whom you are not married?

8. According to the following verses, what are the implications for masturbation? for oral sex? for fondling or petting?

> Whatever you do in word or deed, do all in the name of the Lord Jesus, giving thanks through Him to God the Father. (Colossians 3:17)

> Flee immorality. Every other sin that a man commits is outside the body, but the immoral man sins against his own body. Or do you not know that your body is a temple of the Holy Spirit who is in you, whom you have from God, and that you are not your own? (1 Corinthians 6:18-19)

> You have heard that it was said, "You shall not commit adultery"; but I say to you that everyone who looks at a

woman with lust for her has already committed adultery with her in his heart. (Matthew 5:27-28)

HOW DOES THIS APPLY TODAY?

9. From all you have seen in your study, what do you need to remember in the heat of the moment? How far can you go?

10. Does sexual sin bring satisfaction? How do you know?

What examples do you see of this truth in society today?

11. According to what you learned in Ephesians, how is it possible to control your urges?

12. If you find yourself attracted to a particular person who may be drawing you into sin, what should be your plan of action?

13. Your body is a temple of the Holy Spirit. How will this truth affect the choices you make in your physical relationship with another person?

In this chapter of *Sex...According to God*, I suggested memorizing 1 Corinthians 10:13. One easy way to accomplish this is to write it out on an index card. Carry the card with you, and read the verse several times during the day. Read the verse at least three times in the morning, three times at lunch, and then again at dinner. A couple more times just before bed would be great! In no time you'll have the verse committed to memory.

It's All in Your Head

A companion Bible study to chapter 10
in *Sex...According to God*

For a man, the ON switch for sex is the mind. It's as if a sexual stimulator runs from the eyes to the mind to the male sexual organs. The eyes see it, the mind thinks it, and the body is ready to go.

DECEIVED BY THE ENEMY

1. Read this passage from John's gospel:

   So Jesus was saying to those Jews who had believed Him, "If you continue in My word, then you are truly disciples of Mine; and you will know the truth, and the truth will make you free." (John 8:31-32)

   According to this passage, what are the prerequisites for knowing the truth?

How, then, can you keep from being deceived by the Enemy?

GUARDING YOUR EYES AND MIND

2. From Matthew 15:10-20 (found on pages 195-196 in *Sex... According to God*), what do you learn about the heart?

If the problem is one of the heart, where did the impurities in the heart come from?

What are the implications in this teaching for guarding…

your thought life?

the music you listen to?

the movies you watch?

the literature you read?

the Internet sites you visit?

3. From Matthew 5:27-30 (found on page 197 in *Sex...According to God*), what do you learn about the eyes and adultery?

Is the man in Jesus' teaching casually glancing or longingly looking at a woman? How do you know?

How does the verb tense here help you?

If it is only in the mind, how serious can it really be? What does Jesus say?

What does this passage say that would relate to viewing pornography?

4. Read the following Scripture.

> All things are lawful for me, but not all things are profit-able. All things are lawful for me, but I will not be mastered by anything. Food is for the stomach and the stomach is for food, but God will do away with both of them. Yet the body is not for immorality, but for the Lord; and the Lord is for the body. (1 Corinthians 6:12-13)

What does this passage teach about things that can master a believer, other than the Lord mastering a believer?

In this context, does this passage have anything to do with immorality? How do you know?

What is the implication from this passage with regard to pornography?

THE KEY TO VICTORY

One of the keys to victory, as you have already seen, is to guard the eyes and the mind. How is this even possible? You have already seen some very practical ways; now we will look at a few more.

5. What are the instructions given to believers in Romans 13:12-14 (found on page 202 in *Sex...According to God*)?

How do these instructions apply to our lives today?

Whom are you to "put on"? Practically speaking how can we do this?

What are we to make no provision for, and what steps can we take to accomplish this?

A COVENANT WITH YOUR EYES

6. From Job 31:1-12 (found on pages 208-209 in *Sex...According to God*), what do you learn about God?

How did Job keep himself sexually pure?

What principle do we see here that would help us today?

📖 It's a covenant every man and every woman should make with their eyes. What purity of heart it would bring! What unclouded vision and understanding of God! Did not Jesus promise us, "Blessed are the pure in heart, for they shall see God"?

THE WEAPONS OF OUR WARFARE

7. From 2 Corinthians 10:3-5 (found on page 211 in *Sex...According to God*), what do you learn about the weapons of our warfare?

Are you using your weapons; are you fighting the good fight? How can you use your weapons more effectively and fight a better fight?

8. According to Philippians 4:8 (found on page 213 in *Sex...According to God*), what are you to think about?

We tend to keep thinking about whatever we read, see, and hear. Therefore, how would you compare the standards in Philippians 4:8 to...

the books we read?

the magazines we look at?

the movies we watch?

the television shows we view?

the music we listen to?

the Internet sites we visit?

In the areas previously listed, where is your greatest battle? And how do you fight it?

HOW DOES THIS APPLY TODAY?

9. What do you do when your mind turns to sex?

10. What practical steps can you take to keep from being deceived by the Enemy?

What does the Enemy use to attack us today?

In this chapter you were given a three-step battle plan designed to give you success. It is important that you do not miss this formula:

1. Turn your eyes away immediately.

2. Bring every thought captive to the obedience of Christ.

3. Make your mind dwell on the things of God.

Take a few minutes to discuss the practical application of this formula. Take time this week to memorize Philippians 4:8, if you haven't already.

📖 There it is, beloved of God. Put on Jesus and make no room for the flesh with its desires. You'll be so thankful you did. You'll go from strength to strength, from victory to victory—and if you lose a skirmish, get up, clean up by confessing, and move forward.

Return to the Garden

A companion Bible study to chapter 11
in *Sex…According to God*

 "Do you really believe people think sex is beautiful? Most of the people I know don't."

In her words I heard the emptiness of a thousand generations who wished sex *were* beautiful and yet didn't really want to hear that it could be…because they had never found it so.

THE BRIDE-TO-BE AND HER BELOVED

1. Reflecting on your study of the first chapter of the Song of Solomon (found on pages 217-220 in *Sex…According to God*), answer the following questions.

How does Solomon speak to the Shulammite woman? (Not the literal words, but the tone his language expresses. In, other words, what is his tone of voice?)

How does the young lady respond?

What practical application points can you take away from this conversation?

If you're a husband, what sort of things should you say to your wife to convey the same exhortation and tenderness?

2. Read the following selection from the first chapter of the Song of Solomon.

> Your oils have a pleasing fragrance, your name is like puri-fied oil; therefore the maidens love you.... My beloved is to me a pouch of myrrh which lies all night between my breasts. My beloved is to me a cluster of henna blossoms in the vineyards of Engedi. (1:3,13,14)

> *(Myrrh and henna have a very pleasing, fragrant aroma.)*

Generally, women have a more sensitive sense of smell than men do. What practical application points can you take away from these verses?

What else is the young lady admiring about Solomon in verse 3?

PASSION WITH PURITY

3. Read Song of Solomon 2:1-7 (found on pages 220-221 in *Sex... According to God*).

How does Solomon make this young lady feel?

How does he build her up? What sort of language does he use?

How can you use conversation with your mate to build him or her up?

What do you learn in verse 7 about waiting until the time is right?

From all you have seen in this study, when is the right time to "arouse" love?

BEHOLD, THE BRIDEGROOM COMES

4. Read Song of Solomon 4:1-15 (found on pages 224-225 in *Sex... According to God*).

If this is a picture of the wedding night, what do you learn from Solomon's language?

What is the importance of verbal communication to the bride?

5. And what is the bride's response to her beloved? Listen carefully and learn, for his words, his appreciation of her have made her ready to receive him. This is why she responds this way.

> Awake, O north wind, and come, wind of the south; make
> my garden breathe out fragrance, let its spices be wafted
> abroad. May my beloved come into his garden and eat its
> choice fruits! (Song 4:16)

How would you describe this response?

📖 She is ready. She has not been rushed. He has considered her needs. He has not just desired her, he has admired her, and now she longs for him.

LOVE MEANS SACRIFICE

6. Read Song of Solomon 5:2-6 (found on pages 227-228 in *Sex...
   According to God*).

   What is happening in this narrative?

   Is sex ever a bother? How do you respond when the physical relationship requires a sacrifice?

   How did the Shulammite respond? Did she regret her decision?

7. What do you learn in 1 Corinthians 7:2-5 (found on page 228 in
   Sex...According to God) about the physical relationship in marriage?

How does this passage relate to the narrative you just read in the Song of Solomon?

How does this passage relate to your life?

Does marriage require sacrifice? Does the sexual relationship?

When, in the context of marriage, is the right time for sex?

What would God have you do when your spouse desires sexual intimacy?

KEEPING THE FIRE ALIVE

8. According to Song of Solomon 5:16 (found on page 233 in *Sex... According to God*), what does Solomon do to keep the fire alive?

How does *she* describe his speech?

In what ways can you use this model in speaking with your spouse?

What changes do you need to make?

9. Read Song of Solomon 6:2-9 (found on page 234 in *Sex...According to God*).

How does this woman feel about her husband? Why does she feel this way?

Again, how should we speak to our spouses?

10. Read Song of Solomon 7:1-9 (found on pages 235-236 in *Sex... According to God*).

How does Solomon speak to her? Is he condemning? demanding? loving? admiring?

What is the language of love?

11. Read the following words of the Shulammite in the Song of Solomon:

I am my beloved's, and his desire is for me. Come, my beloved, let us go out into the country, let us spend the

night in the villages. Let us rise early and go to the vine-
yards; let us see whether the vine has budded and its blos-
soms have opened, and whether the pomegranates have
bloomed. There I will give you my love. The mandrakes
have given forth fragrance; and over our doors are all choice
fruits, both new and old, which I have saved up for you,
my beloved. (Song of Solomon 7:10-13)

What words here demonstrate her confident knowledge that she
herself is the one he desires?

What makes her so confident of this?

What sort of response does his gentle, admiring, caring speech initiate
from her?

12. From all you have seen, what are some of the things that can be done
to keep the fire alive...

by the woman?

by the man?

A LIFETIME OF INTIMACY

13. Reread Song of Solomon 8:6-7,8-10 (found on pages 238-239 in
Sex...According to God). Discuss the following questions.

How does the Shulammite describe the covenant with Solomon?

Does your spouse know your covenant is permanent? Have you
expressed this to him or her?

THE PROMISE OF ETERNITY

📖 As you read this you may be saddened, grieved because you
believe you'll never experience the beauty of sex. You may be

thinking, *Why should I care whether sex is beautiful or not? I know I'll never marry.*

My friend, Jesus knows exactly what you're facing.

14. What is the promise of eternity as described in Revelation 19:6-9 (found on page 240 in *Sex...According to God*)?

What hope does this offer to someone who will never marry?

If you believe you will never marry, to whom should you turn as an example?

HOW DOES THIS APPLY TODAY?

15. How does the bride express her admiration for Solomon?

How important is it for a husband to be admired by his wife? Why?

What steps can you take to show admiration to your spouse?

16. What specifically does Solomon do to win and keep the affection of his bride?

17. How can we apply these principles to our relationships? What steps can you take to show admiration to your spouse?

18. What do you think about the idea of sacrificing your personal desires for your mate? What does God think?

19. When is sex beautiful?

20. To sum up, what can you take away from this study and apply now to your relationship with your spouse, or later when you marry?

📖 Is sex beautiful? Yes, beautiful beyond description. When it is according to God, it's all He designed it to be. It's not what is portrayed on the movie screen, the television screen. That is man's version, his picture of raw, animal passion. What we see here in the Song of Solomon is sacred love, love that frees one another from performance, from keeping up with the bodies of others, the passion of others, the panting of others.... This is where you're secure in one another's love and commitment, regardless of what happens or doesn't happen on any particular night.